joyful wedding

A SPIRITUAL PATH TO THE ALTAR

Internet addresses and telephone numbers given in this book were accurate at the time the book went to press.

Printed in China
Rodale Inc. makes every effort to use acid-free ∞ recycled ♻ paper.
ISBN: 1–57954–656–0

DISTRIBUTED TO THE BOOK TRADE BY ST. MARTIN'S PRESS

2 4 6 8 10 9 7 3 1 hardcover

Visit us on the Web at www.rodalestore.com, or call us toll-free at (800) 848-4735.

WE **INSPIRE** AND **ENABLE** PEOPLE TO IMPROVE
THEIR LIVES AND THE WORLD AROUND THEM

acknowledgments

For Duncan Browne, whose love brings untold joy.

Thank you: Coleman Barks, Michael Carroll, Alexandra Cooper, Robert Gass,

Jan Johnson, Matt Licata, Melanie Lowe, Sheryl Nissinen, Stephanie Tade.

the minute I heard my first love story
I started looking for you, not knowing
how blind that was.

lovers don't finally meet somewhere.
they're in each other all along.

— jalal al-din rumi

Welcome to *Joyful Wedding*. This book and the two enclosed CDs contain words, exercises, and resources to support you and your beloved on the spiritual path to marriage.

When we decide to marry, we are encouraged to consider a lot of things about our wedding: What we will wear, who to invite, when and where it will occur, what to eat, which flowers to carry, what makes a perfect bridesmaid's gift, etc. There are scores of magazines, Web sites, books, and even entire companies devoted to these subjects alone. While all this can be incredibly fun (after all, there's nothing wrong with wanting to look fabulous), it can also mask the truth of what is really happening, which is actually quite extraordinary: We are stepping out of the center of our own life and agreeing to share it with another being. We are leaving one family and creating a new one. We are placing our most tender feelings and potent desires in the care of another and agreeing to care in this way for his, even though we don't really know what this means. And, in an act of unspeakable compassion and courage, we are agreeing to accompany our beloved to the end of his life, and to be so accompanied.

There is little guidance for considering these aspects of the marriage commitment. The busywork of focusing on the external aspects of the ceremony leave most of us so overwhelmed that we are only partially aware of the life-altering commitment we are making. Familial pressures and craziness may distract as well. Finally, the wedding commitment is so thickly masked by dreams, movies, fantasies, and the ideas of friends and family that it's no wonder we struggle to be fully present at our own wedding ceremony. Many of us stand up at the altar, face our beloved, and make promises only half-understood. Marriage requires such intense presence and focus; we want to avoid launching it in a sea of outfits, flash bulbs, and hors d'oeuvres. Most important, we want to participate fully in our own wedding, not play the role of "bride" in a movie of our wedding. Through words, stories, meditations, and journaling exercises, *Joyful Wedding* offers support in planning a wedding as a deeply meaningful spiritual event, inclusive of your religious or cultural heritage.

Marriage is an extraordinary act of hope. Countless couples have gone before us, holding the same dream of happiness that we hold, wishing for the fulfillment we wish for, extending their hearts to each other with gentleness and courage. Each time a commitment is made to marriage, feelings of tenderness, openness, trust, and faith are generated; and not just in those who are taking this audacious step, but in nearly everyone who witnesses it. It takes a hard heart not to get swept up in the meaning of this gesture. When we witness the wedding ceremony, when we tune in to the authentic feelings behind it, we release our habitual patterns of thought, even if just for a moment. Something very fresh and genuine sweeps through our minds and we're reminded of what is truly important in this life. The possibility of being fulfilled by love, of offering the very best of what we have to another human being, of being deeply and passionately received for who we are: these are the hopes many of us express when we marry. These are the hopes we are reminded of in ourselves when we witness a marriage.

Where does this hope go? Why do many long-married couples seem so distant from each other? How does the freshness of the marriage commitment turn stale? Why do more than 50 percent of marriages end in divorce? How can one truly abide by this astonishing promise to love, honor, and cherish, till parted by death?

One of the answers is to consider the pretense of romantic love. There is no time of life when we are more susceptible to fantasies and projections than at the time of marriage; perhaps only becoming a parent carries similar vulnerability. It's so scary to open our hearts to another in this way that we fill the gap with ideas about what it can, should, and must look like. The illusions about how our life will change when married, the kind of person we need our spouse to be, the course our lives will take, the kind of home, bank account, sex life, religion we must have: these can be dangerous—if we love them more than we love our partner. To truly receive our partner moment-to-moment, it helps to separate our wishes and fantasies about him from who he really is. To attempt this honesty, this compassion, is a spiritual endeavor. *Joyful Wedding* will help you open your heart to what is actually arising within you, between you, and around you.

How can we create a marriage ceremony that will contain the seeds of fruition for this view of relationship? Included in *Joyful Wedding* are simple, practical exercises for envisioning your wedding ceremony together, creating your own unique vows, and truly opening your hearts to each other, the present moment, and your shared future.

In addition to yoga and meditation exercises, *Joyful Wedding* contains a disc of readings you may find appropriate to use in your ceremony.

May these practices be of benefit.
—Susan Piver

contents

contents

we have circled and circled till
we have arrived home again, we two...

– walt whitman

conscious marriage

1

BY JUDITH ANSARA GASS

There can be a magical quality to the time between deciding to marry and the actual wedding. If we are able to drop beneath the busy-ness of all the planning and arranging and remember why we have chosen to get married, this can be a precious time that may be filled with excitement, possibility, and of course, your love for each other. You are marking the end of one chapter of your life and the beginning of another. Whenever we are able to approach the major transitions in our lives with awareness and intention, we invest the passage with meaning and potency. We each approach marriage with the hope of a deeply satisfying shared life. But we also carry with us the fears and apprehensions of what might go wrong. We have seen too much to be ignorant of the dangers and pitfalls of married life.

But there is hope and there is help. A good marriage need not be left to chance. You can learn attitudes, skills, and practices that can help you deepen and grow in love and satisfaction together, through a lifetime of change. This is the path and practice of conscious marriage.

marriage as a spiritual path

What does it mean to hold your most intimate relationship—your marriage—as a central part of your spiritual path? Imagine marriage as a cauldron, a vessel that holds the hearts and souls of you and your beloved… a vessel crafted to withstand fire. The cauldron heats up in the fire of relationship, because there is no hiding in marriage. Our partner will see and receive the best and the worst in us, and reflect this back to us, like a mirror reflects back the heat of the sun.

On the spiritual path of marriage we understand this hot fire is like a refinery or alchemical process that helps us see and heal the parts of us that brings suffering to ourselves and to those we love. We see how we hold back from life, from truth, from passion. In the fire of intimacy, we encounter places in ourselves and in our partner where we may withdraw or lash out in fear, sadness, or anger, as well as times when we give everything, stretching beyond our imagined limits to love and to be loved. It is our protective mechanisms, our barriers to love that are purified within the cauldron.

When we understand marriage in this way, as an opportunity to deepen love and wisdom, we can learn to welcome the brilliant intensity of the fire of relationship. And if we dedicate our intention and love to strengthening the vessel of our marriage, it will not only withstand the heat, but can help to simmer the soup of our shared lives into a deeply nourishing and lasting partnership.

partner as teacher

You may have heard of teachers of Zen Buddhism who walk around the meditation hall with a big wooden stick. Whenever they see a student whose posture has lapsed, an indication that she has lost the rigor of attention, the Zen master will whack the student on the back to wake her up. In most marriages, each partner will undoubtedly have the experience of being whacked by the other. It is almost inevitable that we will push each other's buttons and act in ways that are upsetting and unsettling to the other.

When others do or say things that upset us, our instinct often is to try to make the other person wrong. In embarking on a conscious marriage, we strive to accept or bow to our partner as we might honor a spiritual teacher. We acknowledge that our partner may well bring us lessons the hard way. We acknowledge that they will see our less enlightened behavior more than others do and that therefore, they are in a better position to reflect this back to us. Rather than running away, falling apart, or becoming aggressive when things get challenging, we make the agreement to do our best to learn from the difficulties. We turn toward the challenge and embrace it as an opportunity for our individual and mutual growth.

My husband and I have been married for 33 years, and over this time have experienced many challenges and feelings of wanting to run away. One of the things that has been most helpful to us is the concept and practice of being spiritual friends. A spiritual friend is one who holds the other's well being and growth as a high priority. We remember, even in moments when we may not feel particularly loving, that we want what is best for our friend. We also remember the simple truth that our relationship will suffer if we demand that our partner be or do something against his will.

When Robert and I first met at the tender age of twenty-one, I was sure I had found the man I was destined to be with. Robert was clueless. If he thought about marriage at all, it was as some abstract notion of something he might do sometime in his thirties. Yet there we were, side by side, forging a shared life.

I continued to be reliably two years ahead of him in my readiness for various levels of commitment—whether it was living together, a joint checking account, or getting married. When we were each around twenty-five, I came down with a serious case of the baby itch. I was ready. I could barely let three days go by without bringing it up again. This went on for some time. I think I was afraid that if I didn't push my agenda I wouldn't get what I wanted. Finally—and for this I will be forever grateful—Robert looked at me and with strength and complete clarity said, "Judith, you do not want to have a child with me if I am not ready to be a father!" I remember standing completely still with my mouth hanging open.

There was so much truth in that statement. In that moment, my partner taught me that my needs and his needs were not separate, that I could never win at his expense. I understood that we were really in this life together. We would have to navigate our differences from a place of true and respectful partnership.

So I dropped it. I rested in knowing that we were together and that Robert was very open to having a family when the time was right. I enrolled in graduate school and put my attention on developing skills which would enable me to do work I felt called to do, part time, while raising a family. This ended up being a choice that has served me well.

Robert sped up his own internal process. He loved me and was willing to follow my lead—once I stopped pressuring him. One day about two years later, he came home after spending the weekend alone in the woods and said, "I'm ready." The choice to start a family was clear and clean. We were both fully aligned and and we have raised three beautiful children together.

As you and your partner approach your wedding, consider discussing what it might mean to be spiritual friends. How can you honor your separateness and your differences, as well as the ways in which you naturally connect? Can you see your partner as existing not only to meet your expectations and fill your needs, but someone on their own path recognizing that we are two unique individuals with different histories, different gifts, and different dreams? We support and challenge each other to grow and be the best we can. We give the great gifts of our love and our companionship and the willingness to travel through life together. We can agree to do our best t o be skillful and patient in this journey and to do our best to listen beneath awkward or unskillful communication for the jewel of the teaching which may be available. When we are on a spiritual path together, we are choosing to learn not only through the joys and ease of relationship but also through its challenges.

What greater gift can any human being offer to another than the commitment to stay and to keep turning towards one another with an open heart?

honoring our feelings

As our wedding draws closer, amidst the joy and excitement, it is also completely natural to have waves of feeling overwhelmed, irritable, or frustrated. We may feel anxious, fearful, or even begin to doubt our choice. One of the mistakes couples often make is thinking that they have to hide their fears and doubts from each other. If you and your partner can successfully share these feelings with each other, this can actually strengthen the bond of intimacy between you. To build a strong foundation for your marriage, it is important to be able to bring both your joys and pain, optimism and fear, strength and vulnerability. Hiding what we label as inappropriate or unlovable often leads to the sense of distance and loss of intimacy from which many marriages suffer.

Unexpressed fears can loom larger when held inside, rather than being felt and released within the embrace of our partner's acceptance. The time before our wedding is an opportunity to begin learning how to become each others' safe harbor from the fears that we all experience. You can learn to be more open with each other by listening without interruption, without judgment, and with compassion. When we receive each other in this way, when we create a truly safe space for each other, miracles of love can blossom.

Another key to conscious marriage is to claim responsibility for your own emotional responses. One of the most confusing and difficult challenges of married life comes when we begin blaming our partner for how we feel. This does not discount that he or she may in fact do things that we dislike, or that we experience as hurtful. All of us are unconscious at times. Blaming others can feel attractive, perhaps even comforting in a strange way. But it actually damages the fabric of your relationship. Our real power lies in taking responsibility for our own responses. When difficult feelings are up, breathe deeply, do your best to refrain from speaking from a place of anger or blame, and turn your attention to your own emotions. Take some space to reflect on the upset in you—what deeper feeling has been triggered? When you are calmer you can usually find ways to communicate that honor the truth of your emotions, but are also productive and will help you learn to better understand and care for each other.

As you take those deep breaths, remember that this is your friend, your life partner, and your beloved. Remember how much you loved this person and felt loved by them just a short time ago. Together, from this place of remembrance, you will be able to deal more skillfully with whatever may arise between you.

Many of us enter marriage without having already developed these skills of listening, truth-telling, and self-responsibility for our emotions. If you find the pre-wedding period brings up feelings or issues that seem too difficult to handle together, another good habit for couples is to remember to ask for help. All too often couples try to hide their problems behind closed doors. All of us struggle in learning to share our lives with another. Talk to your friends, a more experienced

couple, or schedule a session with a therapist or counselor. The meditation exercises in this CD/book can also be extremely helpful.

developing empathy

Empathy is the capacity to feel as the other feels. More than an intellectual understanding of our partner's feelings, empathy is a knowing of the heart, a felt sense of what it's like for them, their hopes and fears, their joys and sorrows. When empathy enters our hearts, two things happen. We naturally begin to feel compassion for our beloved. And our partner begins to feel understood, safe and loved.

To develop empathy, we must be willing to step outside of our experience, our beliefs, and our own perceptual lens. It is common to imagine that our partner is, or at least should be, like us. We may feel threatened or annoyed by their differences "If only they saw it as I do!" But we didn't marry ourselves. Our partner is truly different.

We may also make the common mistake of trying express love to our partner in ways we would like them to express love to us. Early on in our marriage I would often try to make contact with my husband when he really wanted some space. When he was tired from a long day of work and interaction and wanted to be alone, I would try to love him by offering my companionship. Knowing that I had had a draining day I would want to curl up in his arms to replenish myself, I assumed this was what he would want. I then interpreted his desire for space as a rejection of the love that I was offering.

It took me quite a while to really empathize with Robert's experience. But as I was able to enter his world, I stopped feeling rejected. I understood that he experienced my offer of contact as one more demand on his energy. I learned to be more skillful. I would make him a plate of his favorite food, bring it to him, and leave. I would offer him a foot rub, with no attachment to it being accepted. Or I would simply and kindly leave him alone. I always found that he was grateful for the understanding and that when he had replenished himself he would return ready for contact. He actually felt loved by my spaciousness.

The other half of this story is that Robert assumed that I wanted what he wanted. He thought the most loving thing he could do was to give me my freedom. If I asked if he wanted me to accompany him somewhere, he would cheerfully reply, "Do whatever you want." He believed this was offering me the great "gift" of space. But I didn't feel loved by his gift. I felt not wanted and not cared about. As he learned how I received love, he too became more skillful at bringing me the kind of response that nourished me.

As we develop empathy, we deepen our understanding and compassion for our partner in all the circumstances of their lives. We stop responding with the impulse to fix or change them, and we are able to be with them, lovingly, just as they are. In this field of empathic love we each flourish like a well-tended plant.

Here are two practices that may help you develop your empathy and compassion for your partner.

If your partner is upset, encourage him to express what he is experiencing. Your job is to witness by reflecting back what you hear and then to beam your love and acceptance at him. It is not a time to editorialize, analyze, or in any way try to fix the situation for him. Perhaps your partner says, "My mother is driving me crazy. She just wants to control everything and I feel like this isn't even my wedding." Simply reflect back your what you heard your partner say. "You're upset because it seems to you that your mother is trying to control the whole wedding and it feels like it isn't even yours." Then stop. Resist the urge to give advice, or tell your partner why they shouldn't feel the way they do. You can simply ask, "Anything else?" Your partner will feel heard as you continue to reflect and send him love. When heard in this way we often solve our own problems. When he is finished, gently ask, "Is there any way I might be able to help you?" Or, "What do you need or want right now?" Amazingly, this simple technique also works wonders if your partner is upset with you!

Another useful practice is to close your eyes and imagine that you are your partner. Imagine being him, with all the life experience he has had, with his own personality and emotional wiring, his own way of thinking and perceiving. Then imagine going through his days at this time before your wedding, doing what he does, and try to experience it as if you are him. This imagination game can really help you develop a more compassionate glimpse into the experience of your loved one. And please remember, they are called practices because they require practice. If we want to improve at anything, work, sports, music, and yes, relationship and the art of marriage, it requires dedicated practice.

cultivating presence

Many years ago while driving in California, my husband and I saw a bumper sticker that said, "Having a wonderful time, wish I was here!" During how much of our precious lives are we not actually present or awake? We go through the motions and activities of our lives, from arising and dressing to eating, driving, to having a conversation… without being fully "here."

Where are we, when we're not here? Our mind is off somewhere else. We are often thinking about the past, analyzing it, re-playing it, thinking "if only," or "that was good." If we're not thinking about the past, then we're usually off in some imagined future, rehearsing for it, anticipating it with excitement or with apprehension. Sometimes we can learn from examining the past, or make useful preparations for the future. But mostly, this mental activity keeps us from being present. We often think of "relationship" as a noun. I have a relationship. Yet consider how much of the time you are in physical proximity to the one you love, but are not actually experiencing the verb of "relationship." Our relationship is not a possession, like a house or a car. It is the ongoing experience of relating to each other. In conscious marriage, we continually practice being right "here" with our partner. Really awake. Really listening. Really being with each other, as if each moment matters… as if each moment might be your last.

We call these moments of being here together "presence."

Presence is what we experience in that magical time of falling in love, in those precious moments when we gaze into each others' eyes and the sense of separation fades. Presence is always available to us. We can conjure that magic again and again. It is a skill that can be nourished and developed. Practice by sitting face to face, matching your breathing, allowing your inhalations and exhalations to find a unified rhythm. Practice taking turns speaking while the other just beams love and listens with full attention. Practice taking a walk in silence and opening your

senses to the sights and smells and sensations of the life around you. When you touch, pay exquisite attention to the sensations of both giving and receiving. When you make love, slow way down, and savor every moment. These are practices of presence.

CD One: *Preparation* in this book guides you through specific practices that cultivate presence.

It is my heartfelt wish that you be present during your own wedding ceremony. It is a moment of power that will never occur again. Give yourself and your beloved the gift of breathing, looking into each other's eyes, and remembering why you are standing there together. Don't miss a moment of it!

May you be blessed with a lifetime of loving, skillful, and satisfying partnership.

JUDITH ANSARA GASS

Judith Ansara Gass, L.C.S.W., is a nationally known teacher, coach, and consultant whose work integrates a rich background in psychology, spiritual practice, social action, and the arts. Judith and her husband, teacher and recording artist Robert Gass, lead residential couples' retreats in the U.S. and Canada. They bring to their work a depth of compassion and insight forged in the living laboratory of their 30-year marriage. Please visit www.sacredunion.com for more information.

shamatha meditation: the practice of being together

When we think of marriage, we may picture many things: the beautiful home we hope to create, the pleasure of starting a family, the joy of no longer journeying through life alone, even the fun vacations and activities we plan to embark on together. No matter what we envision, no matter how clear and vivid our ideas or expectations, the fact is that marriage means being together. A lot. A whole lot. This may sound obvious, but there's really no way to prepare for what this is going to feel like. You wake up and he is there. You come home from work, there she is. Meals are prepared and taken together. Leisure time is spent together. You sleep side by side, night after night. Usually, nothing very dramatic is happening. As powerful as the wedding ceremony can be, it is preparing you to enter a relationship that is actually composed of extremely simple pieces: eating together, sleeping together, talking about work, kids, vacations, diets, negotiating about closet space, housekeeping, alone-time, together-time, what to eat, how much to spend, etc. Even if you have the most glamorous and exciting life imaginable, the likelihood is that these are the things you do with your spouse: the simple, everyday act of being together.

What does it feel like to "be" together? Often, we think that when we are doing something together (eating breakfast, making love, watching TV, exercising, etc.), we are being together. While these things certainly seem to involve being together, they may or may not include the qualities of openness and authenticity that are the hallmarks of truly being together. In fact, what we do together may actually distract us from being together!

Being together means really seeing, hearing, smelling, and tasting the other's presence. It means opening to him in a way that both includes and excludes your own viewpoint. If you can really be together, you can deal with whatever arises—be it exciting, traumatic, boring, or fun—with a certain kind of pleasure and love. Being together, truly being together, is the noble and impeccably worthwhile act of making friends with each other, again and again.

One way to be together is to simply... be together. Shamatha meditation, the basic act of sitting together, breathing, attuning, and opening to the world around us, harmonizes energy, within each and between both. Most important, shamatha meditation can be a foundation practice for any other practice you may choose to do, including relationship as a spiritual path. Practicing shamatha is equivalent to cleaning your plate before offering it to someone else—and in relationships, we are called upon to offer ourselves time and again. Shamatha helps us offer something good and clean to our partner.

Choose a time when you can sit undisturbed for 15 minutes or so. Find a clean, comfortable place to sit. You can sit on a chair with both feet resting on the ground, or on a cushion with crossed legs. Sit up straight and relaxed, both hands resting on your thighs. If you tend to sit stiffly, let yourself settle. If you tend to slouch, sit up. You can sit alone or side-by-side with your beloved.

The practice of basic breath awareness is taught on CD One: *Preparation*. Doing this most basic of meditations together can be a great way to stay grounded during the excitement and weirdness of planning a wedding.

Practicing being together is a great practice for being together…

– Susan Piver

what we have now
is not imagination.

this is not
grief or joy.

not a judging state
or an elation,
or sadness.

those come
and go.

this is the presence
that doesn't.

– jalal al-din rumi

the celebration

2

BY SUSAN RIVER

the celebration

How can we make our wedding a celebration of love and our beloved, a ritual marking the beginning of a new life, and a commitment to spirit—in ways that are deeply sacred and yet still fun? A wedding is a unique amalgam of sanctified and joyous. Usually, a raucous and/or elegant party follows the ceremony, which is quiet and focused. Both these aspects, the solemn, intense ceremony and the energy-elevating party, are key.

A wedding is a profoundly creative act. No two are alike. We bring our cultural and religious backgrounds, friends and family (some of whom we love, some we may not love so much), and ideas about what a wedding should look like. Creating a "spiritual wedding" can mean somehow finding a place for all these harmonious and disharmonious elements and then going beyond them all to speak the truth of the moment, of your intentions, of your heart's deepest longing, to the one you have chosen, and who has miraculously chosen you, too.

When my husband, Duncan, and I were first planning our wedding, I had a vision. In this vision, we were dressed simply, standing together in a garden, surrounded very closely by our most intimate circle of friends and family. Maybe 35 people, tops. In my vision, I saw myself in lace and him in a dark suit, looking lovingly into each other's eyes, encircled by the supportive arms and energies of parents, siblings, friends. Perhaps a cellist was serenading us. I think it might even have been raining, or at least a bit misty. Someone was marrying us; I'm not sure who this person was. In any case, none of this happened, exactly. We ended up marrying at my parent's suburban country club (the most embarrassing place imaginable when I was an adolescent) in front of 200 people, under a chuppah, to the strains of the bagpipe, attended by my sister and Duncan's son, joined in matrimony by a Buddhist officiant. Afterward, we danced like mad to a Cajun band called Steve Riley & the Mamou Playboys, who made a noble effort to learn Hava Negila for us. At the "bridal table," I was seated next to someone I had met a few days before, the purple-haired Caroline Casey, a well-known astrologer with whom I'd had a recent reading. (We really hit it off, so I invited her.) Amidst the strains of Cajun music, seated next to the plum-coiffed seer at my parent's country club, our vows to honor the Six Paramitas (or perfections, as defined in Buddhism teachings) reverberating in the space between and within us, my father's poker buddies stuffing envelopes into my (new) husband's pockets... I found myself at my perfect wedding, as unique as our combined thumbprint. It was truly the happiest day of my life. Somehow, it managed to honor our families of origin, his son, both our cultures, each other, and whatever it is that extends beyond all these things to make a marriage commitment feel so much bigger than our combined worlds.

Our wedding occured as I was writing my first book, *The Hard Questions: 100 Essential Questions to Ask Before You Say "I Do."* The book came about from my curiosity (and trepidation) about the marriage commitment. It posed various questions for couples to consider about money, sex, home, children, etc: the life they will create together after the wedding ceremony. Looking at these questions honestly proved to be an interesting and heart-opening experience for Duncan and me. After our wedding, I realized it would have been helpful to similarly review a list of questions about the wedding itself.

Usually, no matter what your tradition, weddings are composed of certain elements. Of course, you can choose to include whatever appeals to you both, feels necessary, or honors your heritage. Let's look at each of them, one at a time. I invite you and your beloved to sit down and envision each aspect together, using the following questions as conversation starters. Before you begin this exercise, it may help to take the time to review the questions individually. Use them as triggers to reflect, envision, remember, and tune in to your own and each other's heart's desires.

the procession

Making your way to the altar is your last journey as a single person. In that sense, it's a highly symbolic and important gesture. You are representing your clan and family of origin, joining them and yourself to a new family. I've been to weddings where the bride and groom are accompanied by parents, children, siblings, exes, and even pets, much to everyone's pleasure and laughter. I've been to weddings where the bride and groom were seated on meditation cushions as the guests arrived, which felt very simple, welcoming, graceful. Some couples walk each other to the altar. Some are accompanied in an elegantly traditional fashion by their parents. Some are attended by their children. Any and all of these are "right." What is important is to figure out how each of each of you would like to be accompanied, and by whom.

Who would you like to accompany you to the altar and why?

Does each person's choice feel right to the other?

If not, why not?

Might any difficult family issues arise? If so, how can we address them?

Will we be accompanied by music?

Does what we've chosen accurately honor our individual cultures or "tribes"?

the ceremony

The ceremony is usually comprised of several parts: the opening address or welcome, followed by an invocation calling upon God or any deity, belief system, or higher power whose blessing you seek. Many people then ask close family or friends to offer readings: poetry or prose that is especially meaningful or inspi-rational. (CD Two: *Celebration* in this book contains suggestions.) These readings can rouse certain energies in all present, asking them to open their hearts to the bride and groom and wish them well. If you're being married by a priest, rabbi, or in an otherwise traditional ceremony, it is common for the officiant to make a sermon, offering his or her personal, cultural, and/or religious wisdom to the couple. Most often, this is followed by vows wherein the couple offers their hearts, intentions, promises, and vision. To mark and solidify these vows, rings may be exchanged, the marriage is announced, and a kiss seals the proceedings. More words may be offered by the officiant, then the couple and the wedding party signal the end of the ceremony with a "recessional" or some way of leaving the altar. Usually, the couple exits first, followed by everyone else. This is the opposite of how they came in. Then, in some traditions, the couple is escorted to a private room to share their first few moments of marriage alone. Some questions to consider:

Who do we want to perform
our ceremony?

Will our ceremony involve more than
one culture's or religion's traditions?

Is there a traditional ceremony that
is right for us or should we craft
an original ceremony?* If we incorpo-
rate traditional elements, which ones?

Who do we want to attend us,
either as best man/bridesmaid or in any
other honored role?

What will we wear?

Who will stand by us as
we say our vows?

Will we ask any friends or
family members to offer readings?
If so, who?

If so, what guidance could we
give them about choosing a reading?

Will we want music to accompany us as
we approach the altar? If so, what?

What vows will we offer each other?

Will we write them ourselves? If so, do
we prefer to share them with each other
before the ceremony, or save them?

Will we exchange rings?

If either of us have children, can/should we include them in the ceremony and, if so, how?

What is the best thing we can do in the moments after the ceremony?

*A suggestion you may find useful: If you make your own ceremony, it can be enormously helpful to create a program for your guests. It can very simply list the order of events and perhaps give a brief explanation of each component. This will enable your guests to feel a part of the proceedings.

the party

When Duncan and I were planning our wedding, we were really focused on the ceremony. We made the mistake of thinking that the party was the "fluff" and that the ceremony was the "authentic" wedding. We were really wrong. It was at the party where we first saw our tribes begin to blend. It was at the party that all the energy we had been investing in creating this commitment came to fruition. Today, it all seems like a blur: my mother's arms raised as she danced around me and my sister, our nieces and nephews sliding across the dance floor while the band was on break, everyone smiling at us—ex-business partners, cousins' girlfriends, aunts and uncles, high school friends, brothers, sisters, parents... and, we couldn't help but feel, his departed parents, our departed grandparents, great-grandparents, their parents, and way, way beyond, back to whomever the lineage-holders of our individual tribes may have been. It was pure magic, out of time, out of space; a holy event masquerading as a meal and a dance. No pretension. No posturing. Totally real, refreshing, and uplifting. It is worth spending time considering the pieces that go into creating this celebration that is both deeply sacred and wildly fun.

Whom should we invite?
(This question is deceptively simple...)

What kind of invitation would be appropriately expressive?

Do we want a professional photographer? Will we want posed pictures and, if so, with whom?

Will we have music?
If so, what kind?

Will we have dancing?

Are there any special songs we'd like to hear?

Will we make any speeches or toasts, ourselves?

If so, about what and to whom?
Who would we like to especially honor?

Are there any other people we'd like to invite to make toasts or other offerings?

Who will help us plan this party?

Some of these questions and considerations may seem prosaic, not very "spiritual." But the most spiritual thing you can do is look honestly at yourself and your beloved as you plan this wedding, paying special attention to all the details and to each other. This will help you arrive at the altar together.

SUSAN PIVER

Susan Piver is the author of *The Hard Questions: 100 Essential Questions to Ask Before You Say "I Do"*. Called "provocative and useful" by *O Magazine*, *The Hard Questions* has become a standard guide for couples seeking to make a deeply honest and lasting commitment. For more information, please visit www.thehardquestions.com. She is the founder and creative director of Padma Projects, a media company devoted to creating tools for conscious living.

maitri meditation: the practice of love

There will be many times during marriage when our hearts are bursting with love. Hopefully, the wedding will be overflowing with it, and the honeymoon as well. When our hearts are full of affection, it's almost effortless to feel maitri, or "lovingkindness." We find our hearts softening to everyone around us, friends, family, strangers, even those we consider unlikable. This is one of the many mystical aspects of love: it doesn't stop with our beloved but softens our hearts to the whole wide world.

One of the extraordinary gifts of falling in love is that it can prime our hearts to love all beings. As extraordinary, when we allow ourselves to fall in love with all beings, our love for our partner deepens. Thus begins the cycle of heart opening and more heart opening, softening, breaking open, tenderness enveloping yourself, your partner, your world.

This doesn't always feel good. "Heart opening" has many of the same qualities as "heart breaking." Opening our heart keeps us in a perpetually raw and tender space, as if our chest were turned inside out, our soft, beating heart exposed to the elements, ready or not. It's easy to get confused in this flip-flopped state. We can become increasingly neurotic, demanding, bossy, spaced-out—whatever we normally do to protect our hearts.

Maitri meditation helps us practice lovingkindness in a wholesome, graceful, appropriate way. It teaches us how to be in the world with an open chest and exposed heart, courageous, tender, broken, and powerful. This is a great gift to offer to our beloved. In fact, it may be the finest gift we can offer.

Begin maitri meditation by practicing shamatha for a few minutes. Then, when ready, begin directing a series of phrases, first to yourself. Traditionally, they are:

May I be free from danger.
May I be happy.
May I be healthy.
May I live with ease.

Very simply, you repeat these phrases to yourself, silently.

Then, direct the phrases to someone you love, perhaps your beloved. Whoever you choose, really call that person to mind: his hopes, fears, happiness, disappointments, strengths, vulnerabilities, etc. Once you can have sufficiently roused this person's presence, direct the phrases to him or her:

May you be free from danger.
May you be happy.

May you be healthy.
May you live with ease.

Spend a few moments really wishing for the well-being of your beloved, or someone else you love. If you are practicing maitri together, let yourself be loved in this way.

The traditional practice is to then move from someone you love to a "neutral" person, someone whose face or presence you can conjure but who has no personal connection to you. Send the phrases to him or her:

May you be free from danger.
May you be happy.
May you be healthy.
May you live with ease.

Then we move on to a difficult person and direct the phrases to him or her. You can imagine someone you really dislike, or you can call to mind a time when you were really angry at your partner, perhaps even hated him. Recall your feelings of anger, disappointment, or sadness and, from this place, send the phrases:

May you be free from danger.
May you be happy.
May you be healthy.
May you live with ease.

When we practice maitri, we see that it is possible to love in all circumstances.

This practice is included on CD One: *Preparation.*

—Susan Piver

I take you to be my wife/husband,

the companion of my heart,

to have and to hold,

from this day forward,

for better for worse,

for richer for poorer,

in sickness and in health

to love and to cherish,

till death do us part.

the vows

3

BY DAPHNE ROSE KINGMA

Marriage is the joining of two lives, the mystical, physical, and emotional union of two human beings who have separate families and histories, separate tragedies and destinies. Two individuals, each of whom has a unique and life-shaping past, willingly choose to set aside the solitary exploration of themselves to discover who they are in the presence of one another.

In marriage we marry a mystery, an other, a counterpart. In a sense the person we marry is a stranger about whom we have a magnificent hunch. The person we choose to marry is someone we love, but his depths, her intimate intricacies, we will come to know only in the long unraveling of time. We know enough about our beloved to know that we love him, to imagine that, as time goes on, we will come to enjoy her even more, become even more of ourselves in her presence. To our knowledge we add our willingness to embark on the journey of getting to know him, of coming to see her, ever so wonderfully more.

Swept up by attraction, attention, fantasy, hope, and a certain happy measure of recognition, we agree to come together for the mysterious future, to see where the journey will take us. This companionship on life's journey is the hallmark of marriage, its natural province, its sweetest and most primal gift. To be married means we belong with someone else. We are bridled, connected, attended. We move in the midst of the aura, the welcoming soul-filling presence of another human being, no longer facing the troubling, heart-rending hurts of our lives in isolation. In marriage we are delivered from our most ancient aloneness, embraced in the nest of human company, so that the sharp teeth of the truth that we are born and die alone are blunted by the miracle of loving companionship.

Marriage is also the incubator of love, the protected environment in which a love that is personal and touching and real can grow and, as a consequence of that growth, develop in us our highest capabilities as loving human beings. We are each still and always becoming, and when we marry, we promise not only our own becoming but also our willingness to witness and withstand the ongoing becoming of another human being. That is because in marrying we promise to love not only as we feel right now, but also as we intend to feel. In marriage we say not only, "I love you today," but also, "I promise to love you tomorrow, the next day, and always."

In promising always, we promise each other time. We promise to exercise our love, to stretch it large enough to embrace the unforeseen realities of the future. We promise to learn to love beyond the level of our instincts and inclinations, to love in foul weather as well as good, in hard times as well as when we are exhilarated by the pleasures of romance.

We change because of these promises and shape ourselves according to them. We live in their midst and live differently because of them. We feel protected because of them. We try some things and resist trying others because, as we have promised, we feel secure. Marriage, the bond, makes us free—to see, to be, to love. Our hearts have come home.

Your vows are the emotionally and spiritually binding part of the ceremony. Vows are love made tangible. They both reach from and speak to the heart. They advertise the love that brought you together and draw a blueprint for the love you intend to sustain.

Your vows are more than a bouquet of pretty words spoken in the presence of your witnesses. They are your heartfelt spoken promises of what you are willing to do for one another, under what circumstances, and for what length of time. As you speak these words, you are making yourself accountable through intention—to yourself and your beloved—to live, love, and behave in certain specified ways. Regardless of whether in time you are able to live up to your vows to perfection, what you say here is of the utmost importance; for spoken and witnessed, these words will continuously call you to the emotional, behavioral, and spiritual commitment that from this day forward you are choosing to undertake.

The vows offered here represent both an expansion and a revision of the traditional vows, in that they include some very specific promises about the nature of the union you are entering into. They are tailored to particular kinds of ceremonies presented here. You may want to use them exactly as they are written here, or as a basis for formulating your own vows.

In either case, I suggest that during the ceremony you consider reading them in their entirety instead of repeating them after the officiant. You may want to write them out in advance and carry them with you, or have one of your attendants hand them to you at the appropriate time. Reading them yourselves will more deeply connect you to their meaning, and, because you are making these promises in the presence of witnesses, they will take on even greater significance.

I also suggest that when you say your vows, you turn directly toward one another and recite them face-to-face, instead of facing the officiant. You'll be amazed by the effect that expressing your promises directly to each other can have on the bonds you are making, as well as by the intense feeling this soul-to-soul encounter will arouse in you both.

You that love lovers, welcome!
This is your home.

— *Jalal Al-Din Rumi*

the vows

All that I am and all that I have
I offer to you, my beloved,
In joy
In service
In sacred union.

All that I dream and all I desire
I ask from you, my beloved,
In thanksgiving
In anticipation
In celebration.

All that I need and all that is broken
In me I present to you, my beloved,
For your healing
For your nurturing and mending
For your soothing love.

All that I have been and all that I shall be
I bring into your midst, my beloved,
For your blessing
For your clear reflection
For your sacred witness.

All that I am and all that I have
I entrust to your heart, my beloved,
On this sacred day
And tomorrow
And always.

::

Methodist Ceremony:
In the name of God,
I, _____, take you, _____,
To be my wife/husband/partner,
To have and to hold
From this day onward
For better or worse,
For richer or poorer,
In sickness and in health,
To love and to cherish
Until we are parted by death.
This is my solemn vow.

::

I betroth you to me forever;
I betroth you to me with
steadfast love and compassion,
I betroth you to me in faithfulness.
—Hosea 2:21–22

::

Zen Ceremony:
We nourish ourselves and each other in
living by the five precepts:

1. In every way we can we allow our
deepest Self to appear.

2. We take full responsibility for our own
life, in all its infinite dimensions.

3. We affirm our trust in the honesty of
wisdom of our own body, which with
our love and reverence always shows us
the true way.

4. We are committed to embrace all parts of ourselves, including our deepest fears and shadows, so that they can be transformed into light.

5. We affirm our willingness to keep our heart open, even in the midst of great pain.

Bride:
I, _____, take you, _____, to be my husband, in equal love, as a mirror for my true Self, as a partner on my path, to honor and cherish, in sorrow and in joy, till death do us part.

Groom:
I, _____, take you, _____, to be my wife, in equal love, as a mirror for my true Self, as a partner on my path, to honor and cherish, in sorrow and joy, till death do us part.

⁚⁚

Buddhist Ceremony:
Offering of the Six Paramitas

Paramitas are traditionally described as transcendent virtues (exertion, patience, meditation, discipline, generosity, wisdom). These vows include making offerings as a way of emphasizing each virtue, and an offering table is set up to include the following:

A flower in a bowl of water.
A stick of incense in a bowl of rice.
A candle taper in a bowl of rice.
A bowl of perfumed water.
A piece of fruit in a bowl.
A musical instrument on top of rice in a bowl (a bell or cymbal will do).

The vows are as follows:

We offer this flower so that we may develop transcendent exertion. (Exertion involves being willing to work hard for the sake of others.)

We offer this incense so that we may develop transcendent patience. (Patience is the willingness to work with our own and others' emotions.)

We offer this light so that we may develop transcendent meditation. (Meditation means a commitment to awareness, to working with our own mind and thoughts.)

We offer this perfumed water so that we may develop transcendent discipline. (Discipline, or morality, is based on

a sense of generosity to one's self and others.)

We offer this food so that we may develop transcendent generosity. (Generosity is being willing to share what we know with others.)

We offer this musical instrument so that we may develop transcendent wisdom. (Wisdom involves a commitment to non-dogmatic understanding of the nature of reality.)

Having offered these, may we attain wisdom and compassion so that we may help all sentient beings on the path.

Daphne Rose Kingma is a poet, psychoanalyst, and writer who specializes in books on love and relationships. Dubbed as the "Love Doctor" by the *San Francisco Chronicle*, Daphne has appeared as a relationship expert on *Oprah*, the *Sally Jessy Raphael Show*, and *Leeza,* sharing her knowledge about marriage, love, and relationships. She is the author of several books, including the best-sellers *Finding True Love* and *Coming Apart* and wrote the foreword for the book *Random Acts of Kindness*. Please visit www.daphnekingma.com for more information.

tonglen meditation: the practice of commitment

When we decide we want to spend the rest of our lives with someone, this person unwittingly becomes the target for our most deeply held fantasies, projections, wishes, and fears about what our life should be like. We may not even know we hold the view that when we marry, our spouse will make sure our financial problems are solved. Or, we may believe that once married, our life will become stable and safe… or whatever your particular view may be. It's not unusual when planning a wedding to become incredibly irritated or depressed by our partner's standard ineptness with the checkbook, or continued uncertainty about his career direction, or any other behavior that we thought we had gotten used to. Suddenly and with great intensity, our partner's way of being in the world is inextricably tied into our idea of how life should be. When they match up, we feel happy. When they don't, we become fearful. Our partner's heart and mind may take second place to our insistent view of "what-I-need-to-be-happy!" Basically, it becomes really easy to lose sight of one's beloved—and when planning to marry, this can feel really bad.

Tonglen practice, or the practice of "exchanging self for other," is a radical way of reversing this tendency to place our own wants and needs in the center of every situation. Tonglen does not in any way suggest that we ignore or subjugate our own being, instead it teaches us how to devote ourselves to the happiness of others. This is a great way to prepare for being married.

In tonglen, we do the opposite of what we are normally counseled to do in exercise classes: in these settings we are often asked to inhale relaxation, peace, and happiness and exhale our tension, dissatisfaction, and fear. Tonglen asks instead that we actually inhale dark, uncomfortable, feelings and exhale spaciousness and light. In this way, we are volunteering to share the things we want for ourselves with our beloved. At the same time, we are offering to share our beloved's pain. This is a deeply loving thing to do.

This practice helps us reverse our habits of self-absorption. By working with habitual patterns, it helps us separate our beloved from our own needs (without disposing of either).

This practice is taught on CD One: *Preparation*.

—Susan Piver

at what moment do lovers come
into the most complete possession
of themselves, if not when they are
lost in each other?

– pierre teilhard de chardin

coming home

4

BY SUSAN PIVER

Our world teaches us very little about how to really be in a vital, long-term relationship. Most movies about relationships end after the wedding. What happens after that? How is love sustained? What keeps it alive? We're taught that problems should have answers. Love should last forever. Desire should never wane. Otherwise, we're not suited to each other. These beliefs can cause a lot of suffering.

We all know that feelings change. We can't commit to feeling love. Some days we love our partner, sure, but on other days we may not even like him very much. We can't commit to desire; that will certainly change over time. We can't even commit to being the same person as the one who says "I do" on the wedding day. Yet most of us marry because of emotion, desire, and a sense of appreciation for who the other person is. What happens when all of these things change? How can we still love?

If one can't honestly commit to affection, desire, or even to remaining the same person, what then are we doing by getting married?

Often, we go through life knowing what we don't want: not this job, not this house, not these friends, etc. Just as often, our "yeses" are somewhat half-hearted. We may work, live, and establish friendships in situations that seem to occur by default or are not carefully chosen. We may imagine that our real life is actually still in the future. Marriage changes all that. It is a very pointed, very specific "yes." For many of us, it is our first real act of growing up, claiming our own life, establishing a personal path.

How is it that more than 50 percent of marriages, most of which are begun with this very sense of hope, commitment, and love, end?

When my husband, Duncan, tried to ask me to marry him, I had a very strange reaction. It was a Saturday afternoon in New York City. The weather was just beginning to turn cold and we were snuggled up against each other, talking, laughing, kissing, walking around. We were standing at an intersection, waiting to cross. The light changed and I began to walk, but he stopped me. He held me by my shoulders, turned me to face him, and actually started to sink to one knee, right there at St. Mark's and 2nd. He was about to propose marriage. Just as he began to open his mouth (and reach into his pocket for the ring), I slapped my hand over his mouth so hard his cheeks turned red. In that instant, I felt the weight of what he was about to say, my confusion about making the leap from lover to wife, and a profound doubt about my ability to commit. All the unhappy couples I had ever known flashed before my eyes. I panicked! We locked eyes and knew exactly what the other was experiencing… and broke out laughing. The moment passed, but I knew that the time had come to make a very important decision. If we married, I wanted our commitment to be authentic and long-lasting. But how?

I spent the next few weeks thinking long and hard about what it means to get married. How can you honestly say you are going to love someone for the rest of your life? I'd been in love before and those relationships had ended. What are you committing to when you commit to marriage?

I began reflecting on past relationships, friends whose marriages had ended, couples who seemed to be happy, etc. Everyone I knew who was divorced had gotten married because they were in love. I was in love and wanted to get married too. What would prevent our marriage from ending in divorce?

It was very tempting to believe that our love was special and that it would somehow magically protect us from divorce. But others felt that way too—and they were now divorced. What really makes a marriage last?

Upon reflection, I realized that there was a very important party in our relationship besides the two of us. There was actually a third entity involved in the situation, and it was that entity that could help our relationship succeed, or cause it to fail. That entity? Our life together. As I examined past relationships, I understood that none of them failed due to lack of love. They failed because one of us ceased to love our life together. As a couple moves from dating to a committed marriage, something mysterious happens. Spiritually, they cease living separate lives. Spiritually, they begin living one life together and this life expresses itself through events, beliefs, and experiences that are both profound and mundane. You now physically share a home. The failures and successes of your partner's life become the failures and successes of your own life. A very profound internal boundary is lifted. His religious beliefs may take on a new importance. Feelings about children are paramount. Ways of dealing with money become highly significant. The emphasis shifts from what it feels like to be together, to what it feels like to make a life together. Making this transition isn't always easy; hence the conventional wisdom about the first year of marriage being so difficult. We often embark on this cocreation without a lot of thought, or with much illusion. We assume a great many things about our intended: "She'll quit work after we have children," "Eventually he'll make enough money," "We'll figure out what religion to raise our children after they're born," "He'll spend less time with his friends after we're married," etc., etc.

As I thought about these things, I asked myself if I really knew how Duncan felt about children, whether he imagined we would keep our money together, how long he wanted to live in our current home, how he expected my relationship with his son to evolve. I realized that, sure, in some cases it was very clear how we both felt about certain life issues. But other, scarier issues had been left for discussion "later." I began jotting down a list of questions, and we began answering them, one by one. That list follows, plus some other key questions.

As we discussed the "Hard Questions," as we began calling them, it became apparent that we indeed held a lot of assumptions about the other, and that it was very important to name these assumptions through answering the Hard Questions. Some were really straightforward to answer (questions about work were easy for us). Some provoked great argument (mostly the ones about money), and some left us feeling blank: We had no idea how to answer them. In each case, we learned something valuable and important about each other and our relationship. We continued answering these questions, and coming up with new ones, as we planned our wedding. (I had eventually unclamped his mouth long enough for him to pop the question.) By answering these questions, we felt as though we were creating a kind of "emotional prenuptial agreement." When we stood up together at the altar, I knew very clearly what I was committing to by agreeing to marry him, whom I was saying it to, and what he meant when he said "I do" to me.

Often, people think that the act of examining the details of their life together will destroy the mystery of their relationship, force a shift from a period of great heart and soul to one more mundane and practical. Au contraire! As mentioned, there are two important parts to any relationship: first, the feelings two people have for each other, and, second, their life together. The big surprise to many of us is that those two things may bear no relationship to each other. You can love someone with all your heart and still not love the life you have created together. Or, you can love your life—your house, your kids, and friends, but feel uneasy about your partner. The act of "marrying" these two aspects, your feelings for each other and your shared life, can be a wonderful way to ensure a lasting relationship.

The true mystery of relationship can never be penetrated. We often confuse illusion with mystery. The more you can dispense with the former, the greater access you'll have to the latter. And this latter thing can help create a relationship that will intrigue you your whole life long.

I hope you and your beloved will experiment with the Hard Questions. Here are some suggestions and tips for doing so.

Find a place where it is easy for you to talk to each other. It can be over a romantic dinner in a restaurant, while taking a drive in the country, or as you shop for groceries. Each question should be answered by both of you, one at a time. When you are both ready, one of you may begin answering the first question you have chosen. It may take a moment or an hour. Allow each person to answer fully, without interruption. Each person may take as much (or as little) time as needed. It is important for the listener to simply hold the space for the speaker by looking at him, listening to him, fully, until the end. You can sit close together, holding hands, or apart, across a table. Whatever enables you to focus and concentrate is what you should do.

Try to listen without censure, with as little judgment as possible. As questions, emotions, thoughts arise, set them aside.

Try not to relate to them. Try to continually open up more and more space in your own mind and heart for your partner's answers. Your own judgments and responses, while crucially important, will take up too much room right now. Trust, really trust, that they will still be there when you need them. They will.

If there is agreement, write out the shared answer. "We both see $75,000 as an appropriate, combined annual income for ourselves." Set it aside and move on to the next question. When you have finished answering the Hard Questions, you will have important answers about making your life together happy, at this moment in time. Save these answers, whether you have agreed, disagreed, or drawn a blank. Keep them in a special place, perhaps in a beautiful binder or together with other sacred mementos of your relationship. Feel free to revisit the answers or change them together any time. Life changes and so will they.

It is wonderful when you and your partner agree on the answer to one of life's Hard Questions. One thing our culture doesn't teach us is that it can be equally wonderful when you and your partner disagree. We tend to fear disagreement. Our minds come up with so many stories about what disagreement means: "We're not right for each other." "My life will be made miserable by her." "He will eventually leave me because of this." "I will have to become someone I'm not in order to continue living with her." Ultimately, disagreement conjures the expectation of failure. Very scary.

But if we work with our minds, we can arrive at a place where disagreement means none of these things. We are brought up to believe that discomfort is bad, to be banished, disposed of by whatever means available. This is sad. It's true that discomfort doesn't feel good, but if we can find a way, within ourselves and together, to hold off, even just for a moment, from running from discomfort, it will bear gifts. The nature of disagreement is discomfort—but discomfort just means that a boundary is being stretched.

What does this mean on a practical level? It means taking no position in a disagreement. The moment I say "you are wrong and I am right," the conversation is over. The key is to continually express your own feelings without making pronouncements about the other person's feelings, needs, desires. "When you say that $30,000 is an adequate income for our family, I feel really, really scared of living in poverty" is quite different from "$30,000 will never be enough for the life I want to live." The former invites intimacy and dialog, the latter is an ultimatum. Even if one partner never wants to do more than $30,000 worth of work, he can most likely empathize with the other's fears about poverty. If each can find a way to acknowledge the validity of the other's feelings, there can be a conversation. Even if a couple ends up disagreeing on the specific outcome, they will have evolved their relationship, their knowledge of the other to a deeper level.

We're taught that the heady, exciting initial period of falling in love will end. I agree. But then what? We're not taught that what comes after that can be even more amazing: love borne of being truly accompanied through this life. This love is profoundly satisfying, healing, transformative, and sexy. I believe it's the best we can offer each other as human beings: the grace and delight of truly knowing each other. This is intimacy of a wholly different sort, one we are not taught exists. It's worth a lifetime of commitment.

Marriage is an extraordinary act of hope. When we marry, we are expressing our hope that our partner will give us his love for the rest of his life, and that we will be able to give him ours. We are expressing our hopes about the future and the kind of life we would like to live. We are expressing our hope to be happy. I wish you this happiness.

Most of us believe that because we love someone, we will naturally love our life together. This isn't the case. We can love our partner very much and still not be very happy with our life together. Or, we can love our life—our home, our friends, our community—but not be so thrilled with each other. Balancing your feelings for each other and your life together requires skill and attention.

One way to begin this balancing act is by making sure you really know how your partner envisions your life together, and by sharing your views with him. Practice answering these questions together:

home

Where is our home?

How long will we live there?

How much of our income will we spend on purchasing or renting our home?

Where do we envision ourselves living in 5 years? 25 years?

How will we decorate our home, in what style?

money

Will we keep our money separate
or together?

Do we know how much money the
other has in his/her bank account? Do
we need to know?

How will we decide what to spend our
money on?

What is each one's biggest concern about
the other's attitudes toward money?

How much money will we save each
month? Each year?

children

Will we have children?

If so, when and how many?

How might our work lives/creative aspira-
tions need to shift if we have children?

religion & spirituality

Do we share a religion or spiritual path?

If we have children, what will we tell
them about death and God?

What holidays do we want to celebrate
and with whom?

Will we join a church or other group?

love conquers all things:
let us too give in to love.

— virgil

yoga for couples

5

BY CYNDI LEE

In OM yoga, you are invited to approach your yoga practice with curiosity, rather than goals. It is a practice of quietly watching your mind and noticing your breath, your heart, and your body. This process is called making friends with yourself. OM yoga for couples is based on the same techniques and principles as regular OM yoga—we extend this approach of openhearted inquisitiveness to our partner.

We all have ideas about our partners: who they are, how they should be and act. And let's admit it, at least secretly we wish that the other person would change. These yoga poses are a way to learn more about who your partner really is and to work with that.

Don't you think it's interesting that the word "yoga," often translated as union, comes from the Sanskrit *yuj*, which means to yoke or bind. That's often how we feel in a relationship—yoked and bound.

But the union aspect of yoga arises from the joining of opposites: male and female, up and down, in and out, hard and soft. It encourages us to discover those dualities in ourselves and include them all in the dance of various energies that make up who we are.

For couples, yoga can be a new way to notice and explore changes in our partner and awaken to their potential. Can we be intrigued by the parts of them that are different from us, instead of threatened or confused? Can we be brave and not understand them all the time? Can we be confident enough to be who we are when they don't understand us? This approach prepares an open ground for both parties to meet on equal footing, which is the best foundation for real union.

Couples yoga is a way for each partner to stand on their own two feet and still support each other. It's a way to discover the other person's strengths and weaknesses and include it all in the mix. It's a way to coordinate your efforts. It's something fun to do on a Sunday afternoon.

To do these poses safely and comfortably, take some time to create space and apply some padding. We all know that every relationship needs space and padding from time to time and if you figure out where to put it, you will be able to remain in the relationship/pose comfortably.

When you discover that a pose is chafing, or unbalanced, you can simply rearrange yourselves so that it works for both people. When it works for both of you, then it works. Making adjustments and modifications is like having a conversation, rather than making one choice and then sticking to that forever without being brave enough to examine the discomfort that inevitably arises when we don't let things change.

Here's an example. You might start out feeling fine in a pose, but then after a few breaths, your knee starts to bother you. Instead of taking one of the following approaches, "I'll just suffer here for a little while longer, and then I'm never doing this yoga thing again," or "Doesn't he know it hurts my knee when he does that?" or "Didn't I hear that it's good to hurt? No pain, no gain," try asking yourself, "If my knee hurts, how can I adjust my leg?" You can also tell your partner that your knee is uncomfortable and he or she might ask, "How can I adjust to help you?"

Remember, there is a difference between being trapped and working within a structure. There are always options in a structure. The practice of yoga helps us learn about our habitual approach to relationships.

In traditional Buddhist mindfulness meditation practice, which we draw on in OM yoga, the use of the breath is also a method to focus your mind. Our thoughts by nature are in the past or in the future, and it is when we get caught up in our discursive thoughts that we start to feel disconnected and separate from ourselves, other people, and our lives. Our breath, on the other hand, is by nature always in the present, and when we watch our breath, going in and out, we are in the present. This technique helps us to participate more actively in our own life as we are living it, rather than spacing out and daydreaming that we're in Bali when we're actually walking down the frozen food aisle of the A&P.

When we work with a partner, we do the same thing. Instead of falling into the familiarity we always feel with each other, we can simply breath together. Coordinating our breathing is a way of harmonizing your energy with your partner's and brings both of your minds into the same place and time. Then when you are touching your partner, you can really feel their heat, strength, and vulnerability. You can see the color of your partner's eyes more vividly and become sensitive to how he or she is today. And your partner can experience you more profoundly when you are open in this way. So the ordinary act of breathing becomes the ultimate act of giving and receiving.

There is a Zen koan that says, "Not knowing is the most intimate." It is our challenge in relationships to continually let go of what we think we know about our partner—and our ideas about how they can best help move forward our personal agenda. One way to do this is to wake up to them, ourselves, and our life together through the simple and precious act of breathing together.

In each of these simple stretches and breathing exercises, the two of you will be in physical contact. The points of contact will most likely not be the ways you normally touch each other, so it will be pret-

ty funny, sometimes challenging, possibly irritating, as well as sexy and soothing, sort of like—a relationship! Use the drawings to guide you and play around together to see if you can figure the poses out, or come up with something else you like.

If you haven't done yoga before, don't worry. Just keep breathing. And if you have, then I invite you to enter this experience with a beginner's mind. Let this be a fresh experience for both of you equally. Even if you're not new to each other, or to yoga, this is probably not what you usually do together. I hope you'll use this program over and over again because even after you've done it several times, each day is different. New experiences will arise and there's always more to discover about yourself, each other, and how you are together. I invite you to approach these poses, yourself, your partner, and your relationship with curiosity and playfulness. Let this be a way to practice accommodating each other's strengths, weaknesses, and needs, and still fulfill your own.

The following poses are pictured on pages 70 and 71.

bow

Sit cross-legged on the floor facing each other. I recommend sitting on a cushion or two; that will help you keep your spine long and allow the knees to be lower than the hips. Sit close enough together so that your knees are touching. Place your palms together in front of your heart, look at each other and, in an offering of respect, bow toward each other.

breathing with palms together

Place your palms together against your partner's. Close your eyes. Feel your partner's hand: its texture, heat, or coolness. Maybe you can feel your breath moving together, in and out, through the palms of your hands.

breathing with palms apart

Keeping your eyes closed, slowly begin to separate your palms, just a little bit, drawing your hands apart only a few inches. Stay there and feel the heat between your palms.

calming breath

Open your eyes now and let your palms float down and come to rest on your thighs, just above your knees. This hand position or "mudra" is called "resting the mind." We'll stay like this as we do our first breathing exercise. We'll be inhaling and exhaling in equal measure. We'll use a count of four. To begin, exhale completely. Then inhale for a count of four. Exhale for a count of four. Do this together 5 times, ending on an exhalation. Watch each other's bodies expand as you draw the breath in and down and soften as you exhale the breath up and out. Try to keep your breathing smooth, even, and synchronized with your partner's. Watching each other's bodies expanding and contracting gives you a chance to get in touch with the delicate ebb and flow of your partner's life force.

calming breath with arms

Now we'll add an arm movement to the calming breath. This begins to open the shoulders and chest and expand our breathing capacity. Place your fingertips on the floor, out to your sides. On an inhalation, lift your arms overhead for four counts and exhale back down for four counts, trying to move in unison with your partner. Begin by exhaling completely. Then up and down, 5 times.

cow pose upright

Place your palms on each other's knees.

Exhale together. Now take a big breath in as you lift your chest and face up to the ceiling, making an arch in your spine.

cat pose upright

As you exhale curl and round your back, drop your head and tuck your tailbone way under. Try this Cow and Cat 5 times, ending on an exhalation. Then inhale and come back to your sitting position.

seated spinal twist

Now place your left hand on your partner's left knee and your right hand on the floor behind you. Take a breath in and exhale, twisting to the right. Try to keep long in the spine and include your head so that you're looking to the right. Breathe in and breathe out 3 times, gently and smoothly. As you exhale, come back to the center. Change, and place your right hand on your partner's right knee, left hand on the floor behind you, and twist to the left. Stay here for three more breaths. Exhale back to center.

sitting back to back

Sit cross-legged with your backs touching. See if you can feel your spines align together. Our backs have as much personality as our fronts, but we don't often get to feel each other in this way.

back to back, leaning forward and back

One of you can begin walking your hands out in front of you, beginning to lean forward as the other leans back. Take your time and try to breathe together. Depending on your weight and size you may or may not be able to lean all the way forward. Just go as far as feels comfort-able. Switch back and forth a few times.

back to back, side bending

Lift your arms overhead by your ears. One of you can lean left as the other leans right. You can drop your bottom arm or hand to the floor. Try to keep all four sitting bones on the floor. Together, take a deep breath in and make a side stretch to the other side. Try to feel long on both sides of your waist. Inhale and come up, arms still lifted.

back to back, seated spinal twist

Now, both make a twist to the right and let your arms float down, placing your right hand on your partner's knee and your left hand on your own right knee.

Then inhale back to the center, arms all the way up, and, as you exhale, reverse the twist placing your left hand behind you on your partner's knee and your right hand on your left knee. Inhale back to center and exhale, letting your arms float down to your sides.

relaxation

Lie down on the floor next to each other, legs stretched all the way out. Let your legs separate about hip distance apart and fall open naturally. Place your arms about 10 inches from your sides with your palms facing up. If you're holding hands, rotate so that both palms are facing up, allowing your shoulder blades to tuck into your ribs and your chest to open. Close your eyes and take a rest. Rest together in this way, watching your thoughts coming and going like birds playing in the sky.

spoons

After a few minutes (or longer if you like), begin to deepen your breathing. Bend your knees slightly and roll over to your right side. In this position, scooch together until you are "spooning." Feel your breathing together.

hug

Slowly sit all the way up, letting your head be the last thing to come up. Make your way to sitting cross-legged, facing each other, as you were in the beginning. Still facing each other, one of you can sit on the other's lap and wrap your legs around your partner as you both embrace.

yoga for couples

bow

breathing with
palms together

breathing with
palms apart

calming breath

calming breath
with arms

cow pose
upright

cat pose upright

seated
spinal twist

sitting back
to back

yoga for couples

back to back, leaning
forward and back

back to back,
side bending

back to back,
seated spinal twist

relaxation

spoons

hug

CYNDI LEE

Cyndi Lee, director of **OM** yoga center in New York City, is a practitioner of both hatha yoga and Tibetan Buddhism, and has been teaching yoga for over 20 years.

Cyndi is the author and artist of the best-selling *OM Yoga in a Box* series (Beginner, Intermediate, and Couples), as well as *OM Yoga, A Daily Practice* (Chronicle Books 2002) and *Yoga Body, Buddha Mind* (Riverhead Press, 2003). She currently writes a regular column for the *Shambhala Sun* called "Body, Breath & Mind." Please visit www.omyoga.com for more information.

In May 2002, she married David Nichtern. David offers meditation instruction on CD One: *Preparation.*

to love is to discover and complete one's self in someone other than oneself.

– pierre teilhard de chardin

CD One: *Preparation*

This disc contains meditation practices designed to help couples prepare for and be fully present during their wedding and after. Taught by David Nichtern, a teacher in the Shambhala Buddhist tradition.

1. Introduction 8:03

2. Shamatha Meditation 17:42

3. Maitri Meditation 26:37

4. Tonglen Meditation 23:42

CD Two: *Celebration*

This disc contains a multitude of readings that may be appropriate for your ceremony, or simply to listen to together, just the two of you. Selected and read by Antra and Rich Borofsky.

Section One: On Love

1. from "Music Master" (Rumi) 1:06

2. from "Music Master" (Rumi) :21

3. "This We Have Now" (Rumi) :18

4. "When It's Cold" (Rumi) :29

5. "Art" (Rumi) :18

6. "I Have Five Things to Say" (Rumi) :51

7. from "Music Master" (Rumi) :20

8. Sonnet XLVIII (Neruda) :32

9. from Sonnet XVII (Neruda) :28

Section Two: On Marriage

10. Sonnet XLIV (Neruda) :52

11. "Eeva Kilpi" (Vahamaki) :14

12. "He Wishes For Cloths of Heaven" (Yeats) :27

13. "Variation on the Word 'Sleep'" (Atwood) 1:04

14. "I Want" (Yueh-Fu) :20

15. "Barbed Wire Winter" (Jacobsen) :59

16. "Oceans" (Jimenez) :23

17. from "Poetry and Marriage" (Berry) 2:01

18. "Commitment" (Weatherhead) :11

19. from "Maybe (Maybe Not)" (Fulghum) 1:51

20. "From Love We Learn..." (Borofsky) :44

21. from "The Prophet" (Gibran) :59

22. "Day and Night" (Jacobsen) 1:31

23. "Heaven and Hell" (Trad.) 1:31

24. "For Me..." (Borofsky) 3:21

25. Sonnet 116 (Shakespeare) 1:02

Section Three: On Weddings

26. "Marriage Amulet" (Willard) :32

27. from "The Country of Marriage" (Berry) 1:06

28. "Married Love" (Tao-Sheng) :53

29. "The Wedding Vow" (Olds) 1:04

30. "A Wedding Toast" (Wilbur) 1:00

31. from "A Wedding" (Pasternak) :47

32. "Apache Wedding Blessing" (Trad.) :39

33. "Vows" (Trad.) :45

DAVID NICHTERN

David Nichtern has been a practitioner in the Shambhala Buddhist tradition since 1970. He was codirector of Karme Choling Meditation Center in Vermont and is currently Director of Expansion for Shambhala Training International, a secular program that presents meditation practice as a basis for individual development and societal transformation. David is also a Grammy nominee and Emmy award–winning musician and composer. He just started his own record label, producing music for yoga and meditation. (Please visit www.dharmamoon.com for more information.)

David is married to Cyndi Lee.

We have selected some of our favorite poems, stories, and prose passages to help you prepare for your wedding. We hope they will inspire you to create your own highest vision of what love and marriage can be and to create a wedding ceremony that eloquently expresses your vision.

Marriage is an ancient and sacred institution, and your wedding is an initiation into the community of couples who have, throughout the ages, expressed their faith in the value of learning how to love one another under all conditions—for better or for worse. These readings offer examples of women and men who are learning how to do this. We hope you can hear the depth of their love and their joy in being able to love without limits.

The readings we have chosen span hundreds of years and include some very different voices. Yet they all have one thing in common. They all offer a glimpse of two people being and staying fully present together. As you bring your attention over and over again to each present moment of your being together, a deep, enduring and unconditional intimacy will surround and bless your lives.

May your marriage be a wonderful onefulness; may it be a kiss of differences.

May the long-time sun shine on all your days together!

Note: If you want to have a printed transcript of any of these readings and are unable to find them, please e-mail: spiritualcouples@padmaprojects.com.

ANTRA AND RICH BOROFSKY

Antra Kalnins Borofsky, Ed.M., and Richard Borofsky, Ed.D., have been together as a couple since 1970. They are founders and directors of the Center for the Study of Relationship in Cambridge, Massachusetts where they maintain a private practice. Antra is a Gestalt therapist and marriage and family therapist in private practice since 1977. Rich is a Gestalt therapist and clinical psychologist in private practice since 1972. For two decades he was codirector of the Boston Gestalt Institute. He has also been a Zen student since 1985. Together, they lead workshops and retreats for couples in Cambridge and at their island retreat house in Maine. They also occasionally perform wedding ceremonies. For more information about their work, please visit their Web site, www.beingtogether.com.

These books can help you plan your own spiritual wedding.

The Essential Rumi
Coleman Barks
Harper San Francisco 1997

Random Acts of Kindness
Edited by Daphne Rose Kingma
Conari Press 2002

Attitudes of Gratitude in Love: Creating More Joy in Your Relationship
M. J. Ryan and Daphne Rose Kingma
Conari Press 2002

The Book of Love
Daphne Rose Kingma and M. J. Ryan
MJF Books 2001

Finding True Love: The 4 Essential Keys to Discovering the Love of Your Life
Daphne Rose Kingma
Conari Press 2001

The Future of Love: The Power of the Soul in Intimate Relationships
Daphne Rose Kingma
Main Street Books 1999

365 Days of Love
Daphne Rose Kingma
Conari Press 2002

Weddings from the Heart: Contemporary and Traditional Ceremonies for an Unforgettable Wedding
Daphne Rose Kingma
Conari Press 1995

OM Yoga: A Daily Practice
Cyndi Lee
Chronicle Books 2002

OM Yoga in a Box for Couples
Cyndi Lee
Hay House 2001

Creative Weddings: Any Up-to-Date Guide for Making Your Wedding as Unique as You Are
Laurie Levin and Laura Golden Bellotti
Plume 1994

Weddings by Design: A Guide to Non-Traditional Ceremonies
Richard Leviton
Harper San Francisco 1994

The Hard Questions: 100 Essential Questions to Ask Before You Say "I Do"
Susan Piver
Tarcher 2000

Joyful Mind: A Practical Guide to Buddhist Meditation
Produced and Compiled by Susan Piver
Rodale 2002

The Spirit of Loving: Reflections on Love and Relationship by Writers, Psychotherapists, and Spiritual Teachers
Edited by Emily Hilburn Sell
Shambhala Publications 1995

Design: Melanie Lowe, M Space Design

Photographs: Gentyl and Hyers

Yoga Illustrations: Cyndi Lee

Meditations taught by David Nichtern

Poetry readings by Rich and Antra Borofsky

Edited and Mastered at Heart Punch Studio, Allston, MA

Please email questions and comments to spiritualcouples@padmaprojects.com

dedication of merit

It is traditional to dedicate any good that may have arisen from our practices to the benefit of others. This way, we are practicing for the whole world, not just ourselves.

You may use your own words to indicate your intention to practice for the benefit of all beings, or you may recite this Jewel Heart Sangha translation of The Four Immeasurables, which appears on the following page.

may all beings have happiness
and causes of happiness.

may all beings be free from suffering
and the causes of suffering.

may all beings never be parted
from freedom's true joy.

may all beings dwell in equanimity,
free from attachment and aversion.